Praise for Wyatt Tow

"A breathtaking collection of poems."   —The Kansas City Star

"The power and scope of Wyatt Townley's *The Afterlives of Trees* shakes you to your very bones. There's some audaciously formidable poetry in this book."
        —John Weisman, seven time *New York Times* bestselling author

"A stupendous poet."   —Patricia Traxler

"*The Afterlives of Trees* brings together exquisite poetry of great tenderness, strength, and beauty, but it is also a book of revelation....
a love song to the life force."
        —Caryn Mirriam-Goldberg, Poet Laureate of Kansas

"An altogether extraordinary woman....Her poetic gifts are substantial."
        —Michael Hammond
        former Chairman of the National Endowment for the Arts

"[Her] poems are constantly surprising, and interestingly so."
        —Tobias Wolff

"Go into the woods, which are these pages. These accomplished poems open a clearing through which to see the world afresh. Lucid, imaginative, present, they focus on small details and expand to encompass the universe...I wish I could have written these poems, perhaps especially the love poems—but then, they are all love poems."
        —Laurel Blossom

THE AFTERLIVES OF TREES

Also by Wyatt Townley

The Breathing Field
(poems)

Perfectly Normal
(poems)

Yoganetics: Be Fit, Healthy, and Relaxed One Breath at a Time
(nonfiction)

Kansas City Ballet: The First Fifty Years
(nonfiction)

Yoganetics: Relaxation and Basic Workout
(60-minute DVD)

THE AFTERLIVES OF TREES

poems by
WYATT TOWNLEY

images by
MICHAEL JOHNSON

WOODLEY PRESS

Woodley Press
Washburn University
Topeka, Kansas

Cover photographs and interior images © 2011 by Michael Johnson
Front cover photograph: "Vanitas Tree, Fog"
Back cover photograph: "Tree, Winter Fog"
(www.michaeljohnsonphotography.com)

Book design: Pam LeRow

Published in the United States of America
ISBN: 978-0-9828752-2-3
Library of Congress Control Number: 2010939667

First Edition

9 8 7 6 5 4 3 2 First Printing

to my parents
Joanne Baker and Russell Baker
wherever they may be

Contents

Preface

It once held you in its branches. Now you hold it in your hands, a fusion of word and image, ink and pulp. The tree has changed its clothes, but it is nonetheless a tree.

Trees are transformers. They change the air, recasting the carbon dioxide we exhale into the oxygen we crave. Trees are teachers, reminding us that change is not only inevitable, but essential for growth. Then they show us how — budding, blazing, and shedding everything to begin again.

Trees are bridges, their trunks straddling earth and sky. Home to owls, squirrels, and adventurous children, they pull creatures from above and below into their branches. Their roots are deep supporters, holding our world together underfoot.

Even after death, trees continue to transform and provide. They feed the insects and turn back into earth. They supply the firewood that heats our homes, the lumber that built them, the furniture that bears our weight, and the books that pass from hand to hand through time.

The Afterlives of Trees is a path through the forest, winding through childhood, adulthood, and the illusion of death. All forms are in flux. But behind the form is the spirit that runs through all life. It is here that the tree and we have our afterlives.

THE AFTERLIVES OF TREES

I.

Last One Standing

Ahead of Everywhere

If you should precede me
if you cross the line
after which no shoes are required
if you grow out of your clothes
before I grow out of mine
and enter the atmosphere I breathe
I will hunt you down eyes closed
every day every night every
breath one breath closer I
will take you in breathe you out
a cosmic CPR
on the couch in the car
in the woods in bed
for if you should precede me
you'll be in front of me forever
ahead of everywhere
I turn as I push off
to the word ahead of this one

STRIPTEASE

It takes a lifetime
to shed our skin.
Take a lesson:

The snake slides out
the maple shakes off its propellers
and hair by hair we follow

like Hansel and Gretel
dropping what we can.
The cicada sings

only after leaving
its shell on the tree
just as the poem

unwinds down the page
losing its earrings,
its shoes on the stairs.

Distant Lessons
for Kathleen Seery

An envelope under the door.
Feel the strand that bridges it
to the hand of the mailman,

through the fingers that sorted
it from desk to desk, back
to the author who before he wrote

stroked the knee of his tall wife.
It is the cord that hooked us
to our mothers, the glistening

string of saliva from the breast
to the mouth of the infant
that now tethers us to earth,

the thread of the story
we are all following with interest
and at the same time leaving behind

as a spider walks the tightrope
that trails her. Ours is a garden
of envelopes. We follow the arrows

that lead behind the scenery —
paper, scissors, rock, detour
after detour. The map is before us,

clues in front of our nostrils,
under our feet as we move
our bodies, far-flung continents

that broke off from one another,
woven by the water we are
treading in the polished dark.

THE OAK DESK

for Adeline Woodward Baker

Her elbow rested here
a century ago.
This is the field

she looked out on,
a mad rush of wheat
anchored to the barn.

What her thoughts were,
the words she penned
are driven into the grain,

its deep tide crossing
under my hand. She breathes
through the knothole.

Outside, the wind
pushes the farm
down an alley of stars.

FINDING THE SCARF

The woods are the book
we read over and over as children.
Now trees lie at angles, felled
by lightning, torn by tornados,
silvered trunks turning back

to earth. Late November light
slants through the oaks
as our small parade, father, mother, child,
shushes along, the wind searching treetops
for the last leaf. Childhood lies

on the forest floor, not evergreen
but oaken, its branches latched
to a graying sky. Here is the scarf
we left years ago like a bookmark,

meaning to return the next day,
having just turned our heads
toward a noise in the bushes,
toward the dinnerbell in the distance,

toward what we knew and did not know
we knew, in the spreading twilight
that returns changed to a changed place.

II.

Dripping with News

The Poem

waits on your pillow
and in your shoes each morning.
Behind the drapes you draw,
it's on the empty swingset
that flanks the frozen creek.
It's the towel that dries your face.

It follows you around the house
like a pull-toy, from stove to chair
and out to the mailbox where
nothing has arrived. It bumps
up every blessed stair. It's on
the phone, which is for you.

It's in the coffee you drink
and the ink you arrange
on the page, in the wood before
the paper, the earth that clutched
the tree that grew to fill a sky
where snow falls onto shapes of things

you once made, but can't get
your arms around anymore,
where it also is. There is nowhere
it hasn't got to, in the unsold
seats and the space between tables
where words mix like smoke,

between this breath and the next,
in the blood that runs around the one
block of the body again and again
and keeps coming back to knock
at the door where a man hands you
an envelope that is also it, saying yes, yes.

The Lie

It started small
a glimpse a sound
then started over

circling like a hungry cat
rubbing itself in
making itself known

a child underfoot
a stalker at the curb
showing up at all hours

then vanishing altogether
changing its residence
dying its hair

remains are identified
fingers point to what
it looked like once

but it's already elsewhere
under a new name
perfecting its signature

THE PENCIL

for Emily Dickinson

To make a spaceflight
Take a poet and one star,
One poet, and a star.

Subtract senator,
Insect, rat, shuttle
Engineer. "My business,"

Says the poet, "is
Circumference."
Watch how she hangs

Her pencil in mid-air.
When next you look,
It still is spinning there.

The Elms

We watched them from every
class we could, their long throats

flashing in the rain
while we tried to fit

our legs under our desks.
French with a Midwest accent

hung in the air, bounced
down hallways. In choir

we sang into treetops
till the teacher turned

our chairs to face the board.
We missed the elms,

their bare arms braiding
our voices in the wind.

I sat near the prettiest boy
whose initials were scrawled

for miles inside my books,
notes folded into white flags.

At the time someone said
these were the best

years of our lives. It came
from the mouth of a grownup

who'd forgotten the look
of the last girl standing

at the edge of the dancefloor
while the music swelled

and the elms grew,
their roots deepening,

releasing all their shining
secrets into the earth.

SPLINTERS

Closed. Grassed over with years of disuse:
the track whose cinders I still carry
in my left knee. Climb the creaking
bleachers to the twelfth row, where I kept track
of the bow-legged boy who tackled and was tackled
hours at a time, and never held the ball.
Now goalposts sag with the weight of decades

through which no football passes.
Feel the bleachers against your hands
mapped with lines that branched out
from this place. Remember the splinters
in the backs of your legs. One way or another,
the school found its way into us. Walk
up to the windows. Inside, a field

of empty desks in rows, markers
from forgotten wars. Pull back
and see the reflection in the glass, grey
hair streaming from the face where a child
lived once, the eyes dark remembering.
Take the curling road beneath the elms
past ivied houses, trailed by the whine

of a blue Schwinn, its crooked wheels
singing every bump on the ride home.
The girl in braids is no longer steering,
but the wind weaves the same smell
of wet leaves into the breath, the body
that moves wherever you are
in the lamplight, reading these words.

Swimming Test

for Grace

Watching her long arms windmill
through water, air, water, air,
we know she's arrived, each day
more fish, more bird, more girl.

Stroke . . . stroke . . . stroke . . .
breathe. Our eyes follow her,
the book we can't put down,
lap after lap from left to right
and back to see how it turns

out. *Stroke . . . stroke . . . stroke . . .*
breathe. She creases the pool,
folding us into the blue
that curves around everything.
See the arms turning
into wheels, wings.

Soon she will take off,
the body we helped grow
so long. . . *stroke . . . stroke . . .*
dimming into distance
and out of sight. In the end
it is we who must pass
the swimming test.

The News

Waves broke
their stories on the shore

then covered up
everything they wrote

as I napped all day
in a deck chair

phones rang
in empty rooms

the paper lay curled
on the table while

history was made
over and over

the waves rewrote
and erased themselves

like dreams on waking
all that's left

are my two feet
dripping with news

On Looking Up

for Jim in Yerevan

Clouds fly across the skylight
scrawling their poem on the blue page
the lines sliding west to east
in your direction an ocean away

where men are raising their clubs
to those who raise their voices
under your window by the opera house
Verdi and Wagner give way

to gunshots and shouts the sound
of ten thousand feet running
I send you the weather
you send me the news on the ground

in weeks what is here will arrive over you
the nonstop poem the sky is scribbling
its message uncoded and always the same
look up...look up...look up...look up

The moon threads the skylight
a shaft of silver in the great room
where it and I exactly intersect
craters and goosebumps

The Bank of Mid-Air

After the masked ball
Wall Street drops
its eyelash

into its own drink
it takes off its tights
its wig its cleats

its tits its
bones lean out
the tower window

drawn to a deeper
mirror a long way
down a down-

ward spiral
the stomach
taking the plunge

through the moonless
night in free fall
freeeeeee

no floor no crash no
sound but
wind

THE WINDOW

for Agha Shahid Ali

I sit by this clear square of the world
And watch the changing glare of the world.

Sunrise slowly threads itself through
Trees whose black arms tear at the world.

Headlines disappear beneath the
Sprawling cat, unaware of the world.

A north wind rolls from tree to tree
Chasing its tail of air through the world.

Above the field, a far-off plane
Hums its one note of despair to the world.

Now pink, now orange, the sun at length
Suspends its long affair with the world.

The square goes black. A pale moon-face
Appears, returns the stare of the world.

I know her look, her eyes, her palms
Press mine in doubled prayer for the world.

BANG

A moth flew into Brahms
over the violins
under an arsenal of lights

flew past the black
holes of the horns
flew by the bellies of cellos

the moth near the mouth
of the pianist
flew

through the arms
of the sweating conductor
heading for the cymbals

the slice of light
that opens and closes
with a bang

PEACE PRIZE

The day America bombed the moon
the President bagged a Nobel Prize
it was the day police started shooting
deer in the park because the neighbors
were louder than the deer

too many per square mile they said but never asked
how many people per mile is too many

so they're bombing the moon
looking for square footage
they've got their flag up there
their footprints all over the place it's theirs
the real estate market that just bottomed out
is now sky high

if they bomb it will it bleed
a plume of moon

at night all eyes across all time
have landed softly there
its long arm tagging us back
across oceans soybeans and lawns
through curtains and across the floor a bed
where a child is dreaming
so like a deer asleep a perfect circle
in the sky before the last sound

The View

Right off the new
young neighbors

have cut the pine
blown by sixty

years of wind —
home to blackbirds,

blue jays, cardinals,
squirrels. Pine boughs

fill a pickup truck,
the trunk in chunks

across the lawn,
the bright snow dull

with sawdust. This,
the first of all

they've come to do.
They grip their saws,

step back, admire
the view.

WHY SHE IS NOT AFRAID

Something taps
on the sliding door.
"Come in," she says.

The tree enters, twigs
snapping. It falls
beside her. Next morning

she opens her fist. Buds
have sprung in the creases.
Her toes have grown

into the carpet. When she tries
to speak, wind hits the back
of her teeth, "Shhhhhhh,"

so she tells no one.

LIKE WENDY FOR PETER

New birds show up at the feeder
it's hard to keep everything fed
whether the nocturnal raccoon

or the cat who waits for him
by the window like Wendy for Peter
I am waiting for myself to grow up

but the face in the glass defies me
line after line like shooting stars
appearing from nowhere

turns out I am famous
all the bills with my name
find their way to my hands

with the very same hiss
as waves turning themselves in
to the shore washed up as they are

having gotten here at last
the moon lifting their edges
while the earth turns its slow head

and the cat and I prepare
for what's next bird by bird
star by star world by world

The Clearing

You clear your throat
in the pause at the other end of the line

a clearing in which trees spring up
storms bear down and children learn to read

faces are remapped and soldiers stop breathing
in this expanse you are standing still

half a world away in your tennis shoes
speaking fluently in silence holding the phone

to your ear that shell in which the creature
listens at the edge of the ocean rolling in

on its noisy white cylinders white noise
on the line between us not a word

just years scrolling by, decades
since what you didn't say was heard

The Bench

Down the hill the creek has turned
the color of moon
through a chaos of leaves
you sit and you wait and the woods
enfold you

one by one the animals approach
and if you do nothing
they resume their conversation
silence giving way

to the cardinal's arpeggio
wheeling from tree to tree
the scree-scree of squirrels
the whirring of bees

an inch from your hand
an ant crawls the stem of the linden
in which the barred owl woos his mate
on another hill in another tree

and all the while the cottonwood is talking
though you've only begun to hear
its voice replacing your own
sliding in with your breath
down the path to a glade

where a bench with your name
awaits your arrival
and on it a book
open to this page

Centering the House

All night Kansas
the lungs of the continent
takes a sip of the galaxy

swirling stars and barbed wire
sofabeds and willows
books and doors banging open

signs disappear whole towns
ditch themselves in the countryside
I stir the coffee to center the house

the place our mothers and fathers
and theirs and theirs passed through
their aprons strung on telephone wires

this tunnel of wind this trial
makes trees throw back their heads
and hair on our arms stand up

we're nothing but breath on its way through the woods

III.

The Confused Garden

New Year's Eve

We carry the body
like some inner constellation

Into the new year
shoulders singing in the wind

A map of the past
we thought was outdated

Light years back but leading
from dot to dot injury to injury

A harmony of sorrows
sung in every scar

Beginning again
with the lucent moon

The biggest in years
the breath a knife

Slicing the way
through the lilac dark

You, me, and the willow
rushing in the same damn direction

Combed back by moonlight
stung by stars

News from the Perseus Cluster

Fifty-seven octaves
below middle C
in the belly of a black hole
is a B-flat
which not even the cat
has ears for

a phalanx of galaxies
held in place
by the tug of a single note
for which we are still

falling octave after octave
off the keyboard
down the stairs
under the stars
and below all shining

fifty-seven octaves down
a doorbell is ringing

THE THEORY OF EVERYTHING

In the Quantum Café,
anything can happen.
Zoom in and take

your chances. Pull back
past Arcturus, light years
from the lamplight.

String Theory brings the big
to the little, galaxies to atoms
on the same blackboard.

It pulls the far to the near,
two bodies across the cosmos
and onto a couch

where forces of nature collide:
strong, weak, electromagnetic,
and the gravity of the situation.

It yokes the slow to the fast,
as space and time converge
in a kiss that's off the map.

Strings or no strings,
distance explains it.
Everything looks smooth

from afar. Closeup,
chaos
in a bumping heart.

Hot Flash

The confused garden
doesn't know if it's summer
or winter, whether
to keep blooming or let go
and draw itself back like arms
through the sleeves of the wrong coat.

Is it hot, is it cold? Fallow, fertile,
November, June? Should it rise up
or lie low, and what does it matter now
that the gardener has retired, feet
on windowsill, watching
the seasons change, all he didn't do
waving back to him in the wind.

The weather never wilder or as swift
as here in the garden.
Overgrown and unkempt,
it's going up in flames, sunflowers
belching through snow.

EGG HUNT

There was always an egg
at the back of the month
just around the corner just
out of sight like a child behind a bush
holding back a giggle   holding a surprise
and it always left a trail
before it gave up and moved on
to another playmate   another yard
and now the trail itself
has disappeared into the forest
so long untraveled and the legs so weary
there is no way back and no egg
to be found under the hedge
where the lawn a thorny wilderness
stretches out for decades in the mirror
but in another kitchen a girl in an apron
is singing over the stove

FIRE

It's only the body
It's only a hip joint
It's just a bulging disc
It's only weather
It's only your heart
It's a shoulder who needs it
This happens all the time
It's very common
It's unusual
For people your age
For people your age
You're in great shape
Remarkable shape
It's nothing you did
The main thing is
It's temporary
It's only a doll
In a house that's burning

BLACK HOLE

The hip is a black hole
pulling bones and stars
it sucks muscles like straws
it is drawing down your heart and your eyes
sucking each thought by thought away
before it occurs to you
drinks and books and decks
of cards and upside-down chairs
sucking the toad from the roadside
hummingbirds backwards out of flowers
a blizzard of corn cattle and flagpoles
sucking swimming pools and children
from slides
   buildings
thread themselves downward
country after country falls
oceans turn themselves inside out
planets change their paths
and the sky rearranges itself
around the place your hip was
where once a dancer turned
her skirt spinning out from her

Fitting In

soon I will fit

You used to fit in the sink,
under the desk, and in the fireplace —
where no one saw. Your broad face
fit in every frame on the wall. Blink!

in the palm of your hand

Now you fit nowhere at all,
not in shoes, tutus, boardrooms,
or brunches for ten. The rooms
of the world are small, you think.

turning me over and over

How true, how true. Outgrow a drink
like Alice did, a maze of arms and legs
sticking out windows, head in space.
This is what happens on big birthdays.

light as I am

The Heart Is a Dog Barking

The body is a neon sign
flashing flashing through the night
it is an ocean thrusting
itself to shore to shore
seeking solid ground
where to be and how to be
it is trying to find its way down
a darkened hall the shoe it dropped
fits no one the scarf it loved
trails behind it tries to read
in the lamplight but the words fall
off the page in no order

Once it was the sky and will be again
once dreams have returned themselves
to their starting positions
their small fists tucked in
like the points of dead leaves
their small eyes closed for good

As the rain has fallen and risen
back into the sky the body follows
because down precedes up
how it hurts to bounce to get bigger
outgrow the life it made and loved
the heart so big the beat so loud
the neighbor's dog wags his tail to it
circling the yard barking all night

How It Is

The sun drags worlds behind it
planets at its ankles
it hauls you out of bed
down the hall to the toilet
and into the kitchen where
spoon by spoon the sun
draws itself through your body
this goes on and on one foot
after another through the usual rooms
while stars are dropping off the map
the sun drags the pen across the page
and out the sides of your eyes
the sky spins your tears
into a poem that falls back
on graves of lovers
and gardens of strangers
the sun without fail
pulls the coat of loneliness over your arms
as you walk in your own footprints
until you reach the place
where we can read these words together

CORPSE POSE

Spread out
behind the waist
your picnic blanket

Place the fruit
in a basket
for your centerpiece

Fill the bowls
of your bones
their soup steaming

Pour the wine
into the gleaming
goblets of your hips

What a spread
light the candle
break bread

Spring Cleaning

A strand of wind
Along the spine

Pulls through lips
And into sleeves

Sets in motion
Hair   corn   leaves

The cottonwood
Its wishing seeds

Winter's sigh
Through knots of trees

And folded arms
Of knock-kneed girls

Gives way to Spring
And soon the plow

Breaks through
The hardest earth

Behind your brow
A field unfurls

SKELETON KEY

Insert the tailbone
into the sky
turn slowly, unlocking
clouds, stars,
a rain like no other
the whole world tilting
on the axis of your pelvis
giving birth to a brand
new weather rolling through you
blizzards of galaxies
touch everything you touch
everything you feel everything
you hear you see you
return in slow motion
to the horizon you are
the line between
the corn and the rain

IV.

Turning into Sky

Inside the Snow Globe

At long last you are in
the blizzard behind glass,
this trail of flakes your cape
of disappearance.

Dogs romp on the path.
Skaters twirl on the lake.
Under the ice, life
swirls. The yellow chapel
is forever framed by evergreens
and at the end of the pathway
the scene starts over:
The skaters are still
turning, it is still snowing,
turning and snowing.

Moving from solid to scattered
effervescent to evanescent
takes a lifetime.
Everything is nothing
if you look long enough.

The Afterlives of Trees

1
Trees have fallen every which
way, crossing themselves

as we pass. We break
twigs with our boots,

spider webs with brows.
We think we've come for winter

wood, saws in hand. But what
we hear is what the creek postpones,

singing along stones.

2
Our wagon full, we take
the long walk back,

glance at a bold
checkmark of geese

revising the sunset. Gold
flings itself in our eyes,

the same gold that fills
the fireplace tonight,

warming us twice.

3
Witness the journey of the ant
as it crawls off the log,

passing from fire to snow
and back to earth. Smell

the cedar turning
into sky. No spin

is fixed. Take in
the thought like smoke,

then change into skin.

4
We bind the short
and long of it

to a *t*. Two logs cross
on a grave,

marking time,
our lives squirreled

away. Scribble
on the woods

that wrap the world.

THE ROAD
for BP

To the right of the road
the grass is seared
to a scar. Shards

of steel and glass
rubber and bone
are what you've left us.

For a day and a night
and a day it has rained
this new truth

into the earth. It is a road
we will have to take
again and again.

LAST MESSAGE

All day we watched the scrawl
of your heart cross the screen

like some grieving hieroglyphic.
Line after line you dashed off

sleeping your way through the poem,
the knocking and pawing of nurses,

and the ding of elevators. It was a day
of interruptions. We tried the crossword,

needlework, one bad cup of coffee
after another. Outside the leaves

left the trees one jump at a time
while you wrote your heart out.

But You

the book open
the chessman still
where you left the game
                    left   left
the recliner scalloped
to your shape
in the closet your ties
a cascade of indecision
rows of shoes
at hushed attention
                    left right left
everything is here but you
a lifetime strewn
across a desk
coins and papers
a final arrangement

phones and doorbells punch
through the silence
relatives cluster
everyone is here but you
                    left
in the dark of an open
drawer by your stapler
a spider
has moved her whole family

News from Below

Of the news from the doctor
you said, "It's the slow kind."
Not a snapping of bone
in the fall from the apple tree,

but an undertow,
a flow in the bone
that moves to every cell,
every strand of hair. You reach out

of the river into our gaze.
The wallpaper in its wildness
stays in place, but the floor rushes up,
its vinyl channels foaming with silt.

The Other Side

Down goes the sun
Out comes the owl

In goes the girl
Two feet

Three flights
To a room

Where from a certain
Chair the moon

Via lake
Crosses over

TREES FROM A TRAIN

A silence swells
between your breaths
stilling the smallest of bones
the hammer, anvil waiting
for what is coming

I stroke your hair and hold
your hand, the bedrail
cold on my cheek

your eyes locked in mine
then drifting to a distance
into which I cannot see

your breath drawing
stars from all corners of the night
through the funnel of your throat
louder than rain

a silence opens
in all directions
the minutes sliding by
like trees from a train

and we ride, we ride
past houses, past streetlights
beyond the last landmark
of anything we knew

until the last one
breathing is me
for you who gave
me my first breath
have given me your last

Abyss

You've left a hole
the size of the sky
in the chair across the table

in the chasm of the closet
your shoes hold the shape
of every step we took

through the seven rooms
of a world with no language
but that of moving

on macadam and the miles
of velvet earth before rainfall
between rows of corn

and up the curving drive
until they landed beside
the bed a black hole

you disappeared through
as I look for a sign
of you slivered with stars

your body without borders
nowhere and everywhere
in the wind moving through trees

on its way down the hall
to the back of my neck
in the chill you still send through me

and so I slip into the deep
abyss of your shoes
standing where you were last

pointing in two directions
trusting the way forward
is also the way back

V.

Late Angel

Geography of Marriage

wearing down rugs

    in each other's tracks

        knowing the road

    of the other's back

        which we follow

    as our own follows us

down up down stairs

        through the seven rooms

            the map of ten thousand

                days in this country

          a path of cups

        a swath of chairs

      to the unmade

bed where we

        come to lose

            our way

KEEPING YOUR PLACE

I am your bookmark
holding your place between sheets
while you arrange the forest
from your chair, your fingers falling
again and again onto the clacking
keyboard like rain on banyan leaves
until you double back to bed
in the late morning, encircling
my spine, slipping in where you left
off, finding your place to get lost in
the book so hard
to put down once opened

CLOSING THE WOUND

I broke away   you did not follow
though I beckoned with my tailbone
all the way down the escalator
silence the stair I stood on
folding into itself again and again
the space between our backs
a gulf crossed by strangers
and shopping bags wave after wave
one blue mountain after another
wedging itself between us
our mouths opening and closing
on the dawn the dark the day lost
between our backs bracketing the hours
until you approach at last gliding down
like some late angel with a camera bag

SOUNDS OF THE FALL

Leaves rain from the overarching elm
already brown, already folding their points
back into themselves. They are the new sound
the wind makes, a scritch across the deck
that calls the cat from the next room.

Fall moves in. It is the creak of his chair
as he shifts to begin a new line, the screech
of a school bus and the whine of the screen door,
your knees clicking as you run downstairs
to greet the girl. A breath, ten years, a hundred

pages pass, streaming from our hands
that will curl into questions, pointing the way
in. When we fall and are scattered at last
think of the elm that for a season
held us, so green and giddy together.

THE HOUSE AS POEM

A cement truck drones
under the shouts of men
we were glad to hear it
gladder still to see it take
the turn to anyelsewhere

a chorus of hammers
in room after room
it's music bang it's music
the view getting better
one flinch at a time

the house as poem
is standing still
post hammer post drill
the sound of a paintbrush
licking the wall

replaced by the whir
of the creek the birdcall
sound after sound
points to the place
of no sound the silence

behind the quiet
numberless nameless we
turn ourselves over
to one another's hands
the shuttered moon

signing our skin
just flying through
as you through me so
the house threads the poem
and the poem writes home

There is a Stream

rushing through the dark
window. It is pushing the mountain
in the same direction like a hand
stroking the back of a cat
over and over. It is applause

rising from blackness. It is you
breathing all night in my ear.
It is me in my slippers
sleepwalking down the hall. Wherever
I am, there is a stream rushing.

It moves between wing beats
of doves and flows from aspen
to cottonwood. It is all that is
left after other sounds
have subtracted themselves
from the sky and from the earth

and it is pushing me
toward the eventual waterfall
where you are also rushing, waiting.

THE FOUNTAIN
for RT

The fountain rises from a deeper place
and thrusts its liquid spear into the air
then turns to fall with death-defying grace.

But when we fall, we struggle to save face
and make our way with ever greater care.
The fountain rises from a deeper place.

Like the gymnast hurtling into space
who wraps around the trapeze in mid-air
then turns to fall with death-defying grace,

the falling and the rising interlace.
It's fear that holds us back from going there.
The fountain rises from a deeper place.

It's only life. Summer will replace
what Spring has cost. The tree will drop its pear
then turn in Fall with death-defying grace.

And so we fall into a hard embrace
and push our hips together in a prayer.
The fountain rises from a deeper place
then turns to fall with death-defying grace.

LET NOTHING STAND

between the elm and the boy
under its branches, between
cars grumbling at a light,
their drivers mute behind glass,
hands at two o'clock and ten,
let nothing stand between the wand
of the conductor and the breath
of the flutist, between the wind
and sweating brow of the house
painter halfway up a ladder
against a gutter of last year's leaves,
let nothing stand between holiness
and laziness, between head and groin
from which we spilled into a world
of tables and tight corners and hard
choices, let nothing stand between
the river and cliff and blue
jay that sews them together whose
eggs fill the crotch of the swaying tree
above these lines, as day rolls up
and stars spread out, let nothing stand
between us that doesn't dissolve
with a closing of eyes and opening
of arms, and after arms are gone,
let nothing at all stand that
was once between everything,
whatever it was, the fence of years,
the fence of dollars, miles, fears
of ending the dance, between
the heart that grieves and the one
that surges here behind the elm
within your hands, be still
and follow, dear

TRACKS

Follow the children who follow the creek.
Their bright clothes fold into trees

and they're gone. How you've grown —
too slow to keep up, too dogged

to turn back. Forget the list in your pocket.
See what you've missed. Deep in the woods

the wind erases the way you came. All paths
lead here. Beside you the tracks of a wild turkey,

and earlier, a raccoon retracing its steps.
There a deer paused, perfect disguise,

and here we all are, leaving ourselves
behind. We fold into trees and are gone.

ACKNOWLEDGMENTS

Grateful acknowledgment to the Kansas Arts Commission and the National Endowment for the Arts for the gift of time in the form of a Poetry Fellowship to complete this manuscript.

Thanks to photographer Michael Johnson for his extraordinary vision and generosity.

Thanks to Helen Houghton, Al Zuckerman, and Sandy Choron, hands that helped move this book out of a drawer and into the world.

Thanks to Woodley Press — its namesake, founders, board, and all the disappearing tracks that preceded this book, and especially to Kevin Rabas and editor Gary Lechliter, good shepherds.

Continuous thanks to Roderick Townley, true blue, my rod and my staff. To Grace Townley for deep support and compassion. To my family, friends, and students for their sustaining presence.

Thanks also to the editors of the following publications where versions of these poems first appeared:

Coal City Review	"Last Message"
Flint Hills Review	"Peace Prize"
Heliotrope	"The Pencil"
Kalliope	"News from Below"
The Kansas City Star	"Splinters"
Margie	"Bang"
	"Black Hole"
	"The Oak Desk"
The Midwest Quarterly	"Finding the Scarf"
New Letters	"The View"
North American Review	"Striptease"
The Paris Review	"The Afterlives of Trees"
	"Distant Lessons"
	"Abyss"
Potpourri	"Why She Is Not Afraid"
Western Humanities Review	"The Elms"
	"The Road"

"The Bank of Mid-Air" appeared in *In the Black/In the Red: Poems of Profit & Loss*, edited by Gloria Vando and Philip Miller (Helicon Nine Editions).

"Abyss" appeared in *Chance of a Ghost*, edited by Gloria Vando and Philip Miller (Helicon Nine Editions).

"Sounds of the Fall" appeared in *Proposing on the Brooklyn Bridge: Poems About Marriage*, edited by Ginny Lowe Connors (Grayson Books).

"The Oak Desk" appeared in *Times of Sorrow, Times of Grace*, edited by Marjorie Saiser and Lisa Sandlin (Backwaters Press).

"Ghazal: The Window" appeared in *Ravishing Disunities*, edited by Agha Shahid Ali (Wesleyan University Press).

WYATT TOWNLEY made her stage debut as a tree at the age of ten. While she has written poetry since childhood, she became a dancer and choreographer, directing her own company in New York.

Through injury, she developed Yoganetics®, a therapeutic yoga system that has spread to ten countries. Straddling various worlds has not made for a comfortable journey, but a natural one — with poetry underlying every step. She lives in Kansas, and her work is grounded in its wind, storms, and stars.

Her books of poems include *The Breathing Field* (Little, Brown) and *Perfectly Normal* (The Smith), and her work has appeared widely from *Newsweek* to *The Paris Review*. Recently she wrote the 50th anniversary history of *Kansas City Ballet* (The Kansas City Star). HarperCollins published Wyatt's yoga book, *Yoganetics: Be Fit, Healthy, and Relaxed One Breath at a Time*, deemed an "Editor's Choice" by *Yoga Journal* (www.yoganetics.com).

www.WyattTownley.com